How to play
TENNIS

Learn how to play tennis with the
Williams sisters

DK

LONDON, NEW YORK, MUNICH,
MELBOURNE, AND DELHI

Project Editor Lindsay Fernandes
Senior Designer Lisa Lanzarini
Designers Dan Bunyan and Lynne Moulding
Editors Kate Simkins and Julia March
Photo shoot Consultant Rene M. Vidal
DTP Designer Dean Scholey
Art Director Mark Richards
Publishing Manager Cynthia O'Neill Collins
Category Publisher Alex Kirkham
Senior Production Controller Nicola Torode

First American Edition, 2004
Published in the United States by
DK Publishing, Inc., 375 Hudson Street,
New York, New York 10014

04 05 06 07 08 10 9 8 7 6 5 4 3 2 1

Picture credits

The publisher would like to thank the following for their kind permission to
reproduce their photographs: a=above; b=below; c=center; l=left; r=right; t=top

Action Plus: Neil Tingle 14bc; **Colorsport**: Andrew Cowie 74tl;
Corbis: Bettmann 87c; Hulton-Deutsch Collection 87crb; Michael Kim 87tr;
Alan Schein Photography 14c, 37tr, 38br; J L de Zorzi 15bl;
Empics Ltd: Alpha 86tl; Mike Egerton 87cra, 87br; Phil Walter 14br;
Getty Images: Clive Brunskill 77c; **Reuters**: Andy Clark 86bc;
Rex Features: Ron C Angle/BEI 86br; DCY 86bl.
Picture Researcher: Harriet Mills.

All other images of Venus and Serena Williams © Venus and Serena Williams
All other images © Dorling Kindersley Limited
For further information see: www.dkimages.com

A Cataloging-in-Publication record for this book is available from
the Library of Congress.

ISBN 0-7566-0582-2

Reproduced by Media Development and Printing Ltd. UK
Printed and bound at LEGO Italy

Discover more at
www.dk.com

How to play
TENNIS

Learn how to play tennis with the
Williams sisters

Text Editor Laura Buller
Photographer Russell Sadur

Contents

Foreword

Tennis is for everybody. We're living proof.

When both of us took our first steps onto a tennis court, we weren't much taller than the net. Our equipment pretty much consisted of a shopping cart full of worn-out old balls. We didn't have the best rackets or the coolest clothes. But what we did have was the drive to be the best. That determination has taken us from the neighborhood courts of Compton, Los Angeles, to Centre Court at Wimbledon.

In *How to Play Tennis*, we want to inspire kids to play the best tennis they possibly can. This book is more than just a coaching manual. You'll learn all the basics of the game— how to conquer the court with strong groundstrokes, how to serve and volley with power and control, and how to use doubles and singles tactics that will give you a winning edge.

All these skills are crucial to playing excellent tennis, but if you really want to be the best, you've got to believe in yourself. Confidence is not something you can pull out of your tennis bag—it's something you build with each shot you hit, each decision you make, and every game you play. Don't let mistakes upset you—they will help you learn.

It's also important to enjoy yourself. Tennis is a game, after all, and games are supposed to be fun. We go on court determined to win every time we compete. But if we weren't having a good time, we wouldn't play.

If you always do your best, you will be a winner— whatever happens on court. Good luck!

Believe you can be the best!

One of the most important things to wear when you're playing outdoors is something you can't even see: a layer of sunblock to protect your skin!

What **to wear**

If you look your best, you'll play your best! So wear clothes that make you feel good. Your shoes are probably the most important item—you need to choose them carefully. You'll also need sports socks, comfortable clothes made from lightweight, flexible fabrics, and maybe a cap to top things off.

Tennis shoes

Look for shoes with lots of cushioning to protect your feet when you're running, jumping, and rallying. During a match, you'll be changing direction in an instant, so it's important that you wear good-quality tennis shoes that provide support for your ankles and are light and fit well.

Check out the sole. It should be hard enough to resist wear, but flexible enough to move with you. Most tennis shoes have a distinct tread pattern on their soles to give players good grip on the court.

Look for cotton socks that will absorb sweat and support your ankles. Make sure the socks you choose are thick enough to provide a cushion for your feet but aren't so thick that they make your shoes tight.

Warm-up gear

Whether you are warming up before a match or just trying to warm up in chilly weather, you will need a jacket and pants. Warm-up clothes should be loose enough to let you move easily.

Heads up!

Keep the sun out of your eyes with a baseball-style cap that shades your eyes and keeps your hair under control. Look for a light-colored cap that reflects heat. A cap with a dark color on the underside of its brim will cut down on glare.

Boys' tennis gear

Choose loose-fitting clothes that let you move in all directions. A light-colored cotton top will keep you cool. Shorts should be loose enough to allow you to run and stretch on the court. A pair of shorts with a ball pocket is a good idea.

Do you have to wear white?

In the past most players wore white tennis clothes—many clubs required it! But styles of tennis clothing have changed, and these days many styles and colors are acceptable that weren't acceptable even five years ago. To avoid any embarrassment, though, check whether there's a dress code at the club or tournament where you are playing.

Girls' tennis gear

Whether you pick a dress, a shirt with shorts, or a shirt and a skirt, your tennis outfit should be comfortable. Most skirts and dresses have shorts attached, complete with ball pockets. If you have long hair, tie it back to keep it away from your eyes and face.

Equipment

Tennis is for everyone. You don't have to buy the most expensive racket, the latest gadget, or the coolest clothes to play. But you do need to find gear that does its job well and helps you do your job on court better. The racket is the single most important piece of equipment. Forget price—you want one that feels good in your hands and gets your strokes where you want them to go. You've got to get to grips with your racket first. Then, you can stuff the other spaces in your bag with tennis goodies!

Getting to grips with rackets
It's important to feel comfortable holding your racket. When you grip it, there should be a gap about the width of one finger between the base of your thumb and the tips of your fingers. Rackets have different grip sizes—find the one that feels right for you.

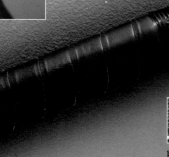

1 Head
The head is where the strings are. The entire area inside the head is known as the string surface. Within it is the sweet spot. This is the area in the center of the strings. Some tennis rackets have big heads, but the larger frames mean more air resistance, and moving them around can be tricky. Beginners should stick with a medium-sized head.

2 Beam
The area on either side of the head is called the beam. You will see that some rackets have wider beams. A wide beam can add zing to your shots, but when you are learning to play, you don't want balls bouncing off all over the place, so a moderate beam is best.

3 Throat and shaft
The head is connected to the grip by two curved sides that meet to form the shaft. The triangular area between them is known as the throat.

4 Strings
Strings are made from a variety of materials. Each comes in a different gauge (thickness) and can be strung to a specific tension (the pressure under which the strings are secured to the frame). Your racket will have to be restrung when the strings start to lose their tension.

5 Grip
The racket handle is called the grip and is normally covered in leather or synthetic rubber. The very end is called the butt.

Tennis balls

Tennis balls are made of rubber and are covered in a mixture of wool and synthetic fibers. Professional players and most amateur players use pressurized balls—the ones that come in special sealed tubes. Pressurized balls lose pressure and bounce after a while and become "dead balls," which are not good to play with. You can tell that a ball is dead if it can be squeezed easily.

It's in the bag!

You'll need a roomy, easy-to-clean bag to carry all your tennis equipment. Pick a bag that has several different compartments to make it easier to isolate certain items (like used socks!). Always remember to pack your bottle of water so you don't get dehydrated and sunblock if you're playing outdoors.

Get a grip

After a lot of use, the handle of your racket may show signs of wear. You can replace the original grip with grip tape. For extra comfort, try an "overgrip" (shown above), where grip material is wrapped over the top of the original grip. Make sure the grip is still the right size for you—if it's wrong it can affect your shots and even cause an injury called tennis elbow.

About **the court**

The court markings are the boundaries for every shot you take. (You might say they provide order in the court!) These markings are common to almost all tennis courts, regardless of the surface. Let's take a walk around the big rectangle together, and we'll show you what's what.

The court | A tennis court is 78 feet (23.8 meters) long. It's 27 feet (8.2 meters) wide for singles play, 36 feet (11 meters) for doubles.

Line by line

There are a number of different lines on a tennis court, and these lines separate the court into various sections. The lines can seem a little complicated at first, but you'll soon get to grips with the court layout.

1 Baseline
2 Baseline center mark (small "T")
3 Service line
4 Center service line
5 Service box
6 Net
7 Singles sideline
8 Doubles sideline
9 Doubles alley
10 Net post

Court surfaces

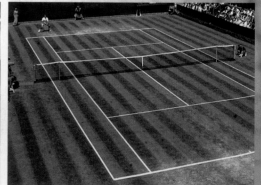

Hard court
These all-weather courts provide a smooth, reliable bounce. But they can be hard on your joints and muscles—so take extra care with your footwear.

Synthetic surfaces
Indoor synthetic courts can be rolled out like carpets and rolled up after the game. Their speed varies—you'll have to judge it carefully to avoid nasty shocks.

Grass courts
Grass is a tough surface to play on— it's very fast, and the balls often zing off it in unexpected ways. You've also got to field plenty of low balls.

The net
The net divides the court in half. A net must be 36 inches (91 centimeters) high at the center and 42 inches (107 centimeters) high at the net posts. Many courts have an adjustment strap to allow you to raise or lower the net.

The surface you are playing on has a big impact on your game. A tennis ball bounces higher on a hard surface (clay, hard court) than a soft one (grass).

Clay courts
Clay courts are fun to play on. They are soft on your joints and muscles, and the clay slows the ball, so you can really focus on each point.

Warm up your muscles and joints to stay limber and loose and to get your heart pumping. A ten-minute warm up should prep you for play. In cold weather, you'll need a little longer.

Warming up and stretching

We always try to make an impact when we play—but not on our bones, muscles, or joints! We warm up and stretch before we hit the court because a good warm-up routine can help prevent injuries. You'll need to warm up all the parts of your body you use for tennis—from your head right down to your toes!

Warm-up routine | A warm-up routine should consist of five minutes of aerobic exercise followed by stretching. Here are some ideas you can try, but talk to a coach about a routine that's right for you.

Warm up

To raise your body temperature and warm up your muscles, you should start by jogging around the court for five minutes. To vary your routine, try skipping, jumping jacks, or heel flicks—just remember to keep moving!

Triceps stretch

Stand upright and bend one arm behind your head as though you're trying to touch your shoulder blade. Place the other hand on the elbow and gently pull across and down until you feel a stretch. Hold for ten seconds and repeat three times for each arm.

Using your racket

This is another way of stretching your triceps. Take one arm behind your back while holding your racket in your hand. Place your other hand on the head of the racket and pull down gently so that you feel the stretch through your upper arm. Repeat for the other arm.

Neck stretch

This stretch is great for loosening the muscles in your neck and can help with any pre-match tension, too! Slowly bend your head down to one side and hold for ten seconds. Repeat this five times on each side.

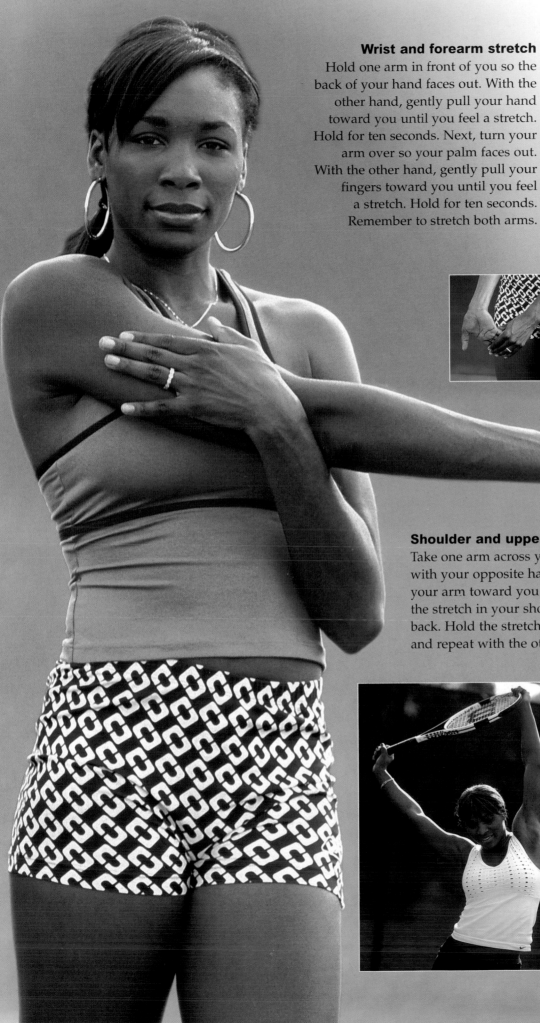

Wrist and forearm stretch

Hold one arm in front of you so the back of your hand faces out. With the other hand, gently pull your hand toward you until you feel a stretch. Hold for ten seconds. Next, turn your arm over so your palm faces out. With the other hand, gently pull your fingers toward you until you feel a stretch. Hold for ten seconds. Remember to stretch both arms.

Shoulder and upper-back stretch

Take one arm across your chest and with your opposite hand, gently pull your arm toward you until you feel the stretch in your shoulder and upper back. Hold the stretch for ten seconds and repeat with the other arm.

Tips:

Warm up before you start stretching—warm muscles stretch more readily.

Ease yourself into your stretches. Don't bounce or you'll risk pulling a muscle.

To avoid aching muscles, remember to stretch *after* your match or practice, as well as before.

Never overstretch your muscles. You should feel the stretch but it should never be painful. If you feel any pain you must stop.

Lower-body stretches

In tennis you have to move fast and change direction quickly, so your legs take a lot of punishment during a match. That's why you should always stretch your leg muscles properly—before and after you play. Stretching your legs is just as important as stretching your tennis arm and can help you avoid lots of aches and pains and injuries!

Lower-body routine | **After you've warmed up and finished your upper body stretches, you can try these exercises so your legs are flexible.**

Inner-thigh stretch

Stand with your feet apart, toes pointing forward. Keep one leg straight and bend the other. Move your weight onto the bent leg and lower your body, keeping both feet flat on the ground. Hold for ten seconds. Repeat, then switch sides.

Calf stretch

Hold on to a bench or the top of the net. Keep one leg back and straight, the other forward and bent. Transfer your weight onto the forward leg, keeping the other foot flat on the ground. Hold for ten seconds. Switch to your other leg and repeat.

Quad stretch

To stretch your quadriceps muscles at the front of your thighs, hold on to a net post or bench to support yourself. Then reach behind you, grab an ankle, and gently pull it toward your bottom. Hold the stretch for ten seconds. Repeat this five times before you switch legs.

Ankle stretch

To relax your ankles, raise one leg in front of you and slowly circle your ankle ten times. Change direction, repeat, and then change feet.

Don't expect to be able to touch your toes. It takes time before you are as flexible as we are. Just reach as far as is comfortable for you.

Good posture helps you to balance, so keep your head up and your back straight.

Hamstring stretch

Stand with your feet shoulder-width apart and step forward with your left leg. Your left foot should point forward while the right one points out to the right. Bend forward and try to touch your left ankle. Hold for ten seconds and then switch legs. You should feel the stretch in the hamstrings in the back of your front leg.

Lunges

From a standing position, place your hands on your hips, step forward with your right leg, and bend your knee. Keeping the heel of your left foot slightly off the ground, bend your left leg and lower your knee slowly toward the ground. Hold for ten seconds and repeat with the other leg.

If you need some support when you are lunging, you can place your hands on your thigh.

Basic rules

For most beginners, the rules of tennis and the scoring system can seem a bit confusing at first. But it's really quite simple: you have to win more points than your opponent to beat them; you win the point if your opponent makes a mistake or can't return your shot. Tennis has its own unique way of scoring (love, 15, 30, 40, game, set, and match). Once you figure out the terminology, though, scoring is pretty straightforward.

Game, set, and match

A match is a contest between two players (or two teams of doubles). To win a match, you must win the best out of three sets (some men's matches are played over five sets). To win a set, you've got to be the first player to win six games with a lead of two games over your opponent. To win a game, you need to be the first person to win at least four points, with a lead of two points over your opponent. To win a point, you've got to keep the ball in play the longest.

The basics

Each point starts when one player serves. If the ball bounces in your opponent's service box but they can't reach it, the server gets a point. If the serve is returned, the point continues until somebody makes a mistake. If you hit the ball into the net, or the ball bounces outside the boundary lines, you lose the point. If you hit the ball within the boundary lines, and the other player can't return it before it bounces twice, the point is yours.

Scoring points

Both players (or doubles teams) start off each game with zero, which is called "love." (It is thought that "love" comes from the French word *l'oeuf*, which means "egg," because an egg is shaped a bit like a zero!) If you win the first point, you score 15. If you win the second point, you score 30. The next point you win makes your score 40, and one more point wins the game (as long as you have won at least two more points than your opponent).

Keeping score

When we compete, the umpire calls out the score after every point. But when you play, you'll probably need to call the score. It's the server's job to make the call, and their score is always given first, followed by their opponent's score. For example, if you serve and win the first point, you say, "15–love." If you serve and lose, it's "love–15," and so on. Sometimes there is a scoreboard to help you keep track.

If there is a dispute over the score, you usually go back to the last agreed score.

Deuce

If both players have reached 40 in a game, the score is called "deuce" (thought to be from the French *à deux*, meaning "pair"). The only way to break out of deuce and win the game is to take two points in a row: the advantage point, then the game point. The first player who scores a point after deuce wins the advantage point. If the player with the advantage wins the next point, the game point, they win the game. If the player with the advantage loses the game point, the score reverts back to deuce.

Get set!

The first player to win six games, at least two games ahead of their opponent, wins the set. For example, if you win six games, and your opponent wins four, you've won the set, 6–4. Sometimes you and your opponent are so evenly matched that neither of you can win those two clear games to clinch the set. You can't go on playing forever, so if the score is locked at 6–6, you can play a tiebreaker (*see* below) to determine the winner.

Tiebreaker

This game is played when the set is tied at six games all (except in the final set of some tournaments). A tiebreaker has its own rules: players usually play twelve points and the first player to win seven points (and who is at least two points ahead of the other player) takes the game and the set. If neither player is two points ahead of the other, the tiebreaker continues until someone is. The points in a tiebreaker are simply one, two, three, four, and so on. The server's score is called first.

Basic skills

Speed, agility, and fast reaction times are essential for playing tennis at every level. Correct footwork and good balance are key to hitting a tennis ball with power and accuracy. All tennis pros include exercises in their training programs that develop these basic skills. So get practicing—you'll be amazed at how much your game improves!

Picking up a ball may seem easy, but doing it quickly tests the basic skills needed in tennis.

Rolling the ball
Here's an exercise to improve your agility and reaction times. The coach rolls the ball to you, and you have to trap it with one hand and roll it back. The ball will be rolled fast and in different directions, so you have to be ready to move quickly to your left, right, or center.

This ball is great for drills, but don't try playing tennis with it!

Touching the lines
To help improve your speed and agility, try this exercise. From the net, run as fast as you can to the service line. Touch the line, and then run back to the net. Next, sprint to the baseline, touch it, and sprint back to the net. Repeat five times.

Crazy-ball game
This weird-shaped ball—that bounces all over the place—is no good for playing tennis, but it's great for developing fast reactions and hand–eye coordination. With a partner, bounce the ball to each other, trying to catch it in one hand.

Ski jumps

With feet together, jump from one side of a line to the other without stepping on the line. Try to do as many jumps as you can in a minute. This exercise improves agility around the court and overall fitness. It is also good for encouraging accuracy and precision.

Jump quickly from side to side but make sure you don't step on the line. Accuracy is as important as speed.

Alley hops

Use the doubles alley in this exercise to help develop nifty footwork and improve agility. With your feet wide apart, jump from one foot to the other, landing on one sideline, then the other. This drill is also a good test of balance. If you put your hands behind your back, you will have to rely on controlling your legs rather than using your arms to help you balance.

Back to basics

Learning how to play tennis is challenging. You've got to put in lots of practice time, which can seem repetitive or even boring. We felt the same way when we were learning. But you need to keep things lively so you don't lose interest. Try to incorporate a drill or two into your regular practice routine. Having fun will help keep you interested in tennis, and you'll enhance your skills at the same time.

Handling the racket

The way you hold your racket—the grip—has a huge effect on any stroke you make. There are three basic forehand grips you need to learn—the eastern grip, the continental grip, and the western grip. There are dozens of variations on these three grips: one-handed or two-handed, forehand (*see* pages 28–29) or backhand (*see* pages 30–31), and grips that are somewhere in between two of the basic grips. Focus on the basics, and with experience, you can build from there.

Which grip?

We change our grips all the time during play, because some grips are better for some shots. If every ball was hit to you in the same way and to the same place, you could return it using the same grip. But tennis just isn't like that. You never know what's coming, so you've got to be ready to change grips.

Basic forehand grips

Eastern grip

This grip comes naturally to most players. Shake hands with the racket, with the heel of your hand at the butt end. The "V" of your thumb and index finger should be on the right edge of the handle, and you should see a good deal of your thumb. Keep your palm behind the handle and your index finger up the handle for the best support.

Continental grip

Most pros use this grip when they serve. Start with an eastern grip and turn the racket slightly clockwise. The "V" made by your thumb and finger should sit on the right edge of the handle. Spread your fingers out slightly, so the thumb rests on the side of the racket and the bottom knuckle of your index finger lies right on top of the racket.

Western grip

This is a tough one for beginners, but after you've tried the eastern and continental grips, give it a shot. It really provides punch for forehand strokes. Start with an eastern grip, then loosen up and turn the racket counterclockwise. The "V" of your thumb should point way to the right, and your wrist will bend backward.

If you are left-handed, follow the same instructions for each grip using your left hand. The right edge of the racket becomes the left edge, and the left edge becomes the right.

Semi-western grip

This is a modified version of the western grip used for adding spin (*see* pages 54–55) or hitting high-bouncing balls. The "V" between your finger and thumb should be on the right edge of the racket handle. Wrap your thumb right around the handle.

Grip variations

Double-handed eastern backhand grip

If you need a little extra stability, use a two-handed grip. You won't be able to stretch so far for the ball, but what you lose in reach, you gain in stability. Place your playing hand in an eastern forehand grip at the butt end of the racket, and add the other hand above it, using the same grip.

Eastern backhand grip

When you want to add spin or slice (*see* pages 54–55), try the eastern backhand grip. The "V" should be on the left edge of the racket handle. Inch your first finger up the handle and rest its knuckle against the upper left edge of the racket. Wrap your thumb around the handle for extra strength.

Forehand drive

There are two types of groundstrokes—the forehand and backhand drive. Both are played after the ball has bounced once. The forehand drive is the shot you will learn first. Many players start with a two-handed forehand and move onto the one-handed shot when they are stronger.

Practice makes perfect

In 1997, I (Serena) injured my left wrist, but I made that pain my gain. I had to focus on my forehand groundstroke while my wrist recovered. Within a few months, my forehand drive was ferocious, and this helped improve my entire game.

Forehand drive | **With practice, the forehand groundstroke can be developed into a lethal weapon. Try these steps to develop a more consistent, reliable forehand drive.**

1 Stand with your feet about shoulder-width apart and your knees slightly bent. Keep your eyes on the ball, so you'll be ready to react quickly.

2 Turn your shoulders to the right. Take the racket back above shoulder height as you step forward with your front foot. Keep your knees slightly bent for balance.

3 Watch the ball carefully and begin your swing. Rotate your shoulders as you swing. Use your non-racket arm to help you balance. Keep your racket arm relaxed.

A square, or closed, stance (above) and an open stance (left).

As you follow through, bring your back foot forward to help you balance. Keep the leg bent slightly so you can push off quickly for the next shot.

Stance

An open stance gives you power through the hips and shoulders, and you can recover quickly from the shot. A square, or closed, stance can be harder on the knees.

4 Hit the ball when it is in front of your body so your arm can swing freely. Keep rotating your shoulders as you swing. The stroke should move from low to high.

5 Follow through with your racket, so you finish the stroke with the racket over your other shoulder. Watch the ball.

Backhand drive

Tennis is not a one-sided game, and eventually the ball is going to be hit to the opposite of your forehand—your backhand. Although some players find this stroke slightly tricky at first, it is important to develop a great backhand. It pays to be equally strong on both sides of the court.

Get back
The backhand drive is a swinging shot. It may take some time before it becomes second nature—you'll need to get used to working on your opposite side, and your muscle strength needs to develop, too. Don't give up, though—once you find your backhand, you'll wonder how you ever played without it.

Backhand drive | The backhand drive can be a little harder to master than the forehand drive, so make sure you follow these steps and practice it as often as you can.

1 Stand with your feet about shoulder-width apart and your knees slightly bent, with your racket at about waist height. Hold it with a double-handed grip. Watch the ball carefully.

2 When you see that the ball is coming to your backhand side, turn your shoulders to the side and take the racket back. Your weight should be on your back foot (your left if you are right-handed, your right if you are left-handed).

3 Step into the ball. If you're right-handed, step forward with your right foot as your left foot pivots. Left-handed players should step forward with the left foot. Keep your eyes on the ball.

One hand or two?
You can hit a backhand shot with two hands on the grip or with one. We use a two-handed grip because it gives us more control, especially when returning serve. A one-handed shot gives you a longer reach, though. Try both grips out and decide which is best for you.

Make your swing steady and smooth.

5 Swing the racket up from hip height until it is over your shoulder. Follow through, keeping both hands on the racket and pointing your elbow in the direction you want the ball to go.

4 Lead with your shoulders and swing smoothly to meet the ball. Stretch out your arms so the racket makes contact with the ball in front of your body, at about hip level. Grip your racket firmly.

The ready position

You should stand in the ready position while waiting for your opponent to hit the ball. This enables you to move speedily to any place on the court. Reacting quickly to your opponent's shot greatly improves your chances of returning it with a winning stroke. You must be able to reach the ball and play your shot as quickly as possible.

Keep your head up and your eyes firmly fixed on the ball.

Hold the racket lightly so that you are ready to change grips to hit a backhand or a forehand.

Your body weight should be on the balls of your feet so you are ready to move in any direction.

Ready to return
Players always stand in the ready position when they are waiting to return serve. Hold the racket out in front of you with both hands on the grip. Keep your feet shoulder-width apart and your legs bent. The lower you crouch, the quicker you will be able to spring forward into the ball.

Keep moving
Many pros don't stay still in the ready position but swing from side to side or bounce. This keeps the mind and body alert and tells your opponent that you are ready to anticipate their shot or serve.

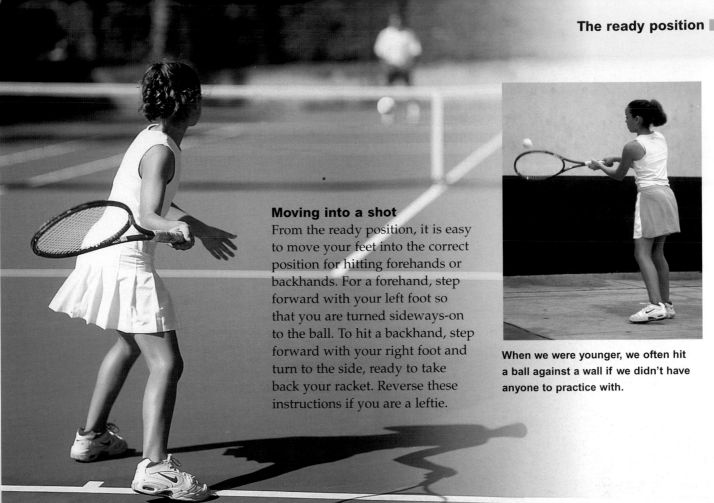

Moving into a shot

From the ready position, it is easy to move your feet into the correct position for hitting forehands or backhands. For a forehand, step forward with your left foot so that you are turned sideways-on to the ball. To hit a backhand, step forward with your right foot and turn to the side, ready to take back your racket. Reverse these instructions if you are a leftie.

When we were younger, we often hit a ball against a wall if we didn't have anyone to practice with.

1 The split-step is similar to the ready position but includes a jumping action. It is also called the ready hop and is used to prepare yourself while your opponent hits the ball. It also helps you regain your balance after moving forward.

2 Stand with your feet shoulder-width apart and your knees slightly bent. You should hold your racket in two hands in front of your body. The key to this position is to keep on your toes. Watch the ball and be ready to jump.

3 As your opponent hits the ball, jump up. This will allow you to move in any position to hit any shot. The split-step is most often used as you approach the net to hit a volley.

The **serve**

A great service, or serve, is your first chance at winning every point, so give it everything you've got. It's the most important stroke to master in tennis—if you don't put your first or second serve in place, the point is over and gone for good. Work hard at your serve to perfect it and direct it, and you'll get a winning edge to your game.

Serve it up

The key to a great serve is consistency—and the key to consistency is practice. Learn to toss the ball into an easy place to hit, get your racket into a good position, and make solid contact with the ball to get your serve where you want it to go. Then make it a habit!

Serve sequence | **Use this step-by-step sequence as a guide. Be persistent in practice until you develop a smooth serve you can repeat over and over again.**

1 Stand at the baseline, just to the right of the center mark, facing the net. Take a step back with your right leg, turning your body side-on to the net as you move. Keep your grip comfortable and relaxed.

2 Begin to raise the ball. Get a target in your sights and commit to the serve you want to hit. As you take your racket arm back, keep it away from the side of your body. Most of your body weight should be on the back foot.

3 Throw the ball gently into the air when your arm is fully extended. You'll need to get the ball high enough to hit, at about an arm's length in front of you. A good toss should send the ball just slightly beyond the reach of your racket.

Service with a smile

When you've perfected your serve, it should feel as if you are throwing your racket at the ball. You'll want to learn a few ways to mix up your service to keep your opponents on their toes. Adding extra power enables you to blow the ball right by some players. Learning how to put a little spin in your serve will keep others on the run.

Tips:

Aim for the precise spot you want your serve to hit.

As you toss the ball in the air, your palm should be facing up. Cradle the ball in your fingertips as you release it—don't squeeze it.

Lift up on your toes as you reach into your serve.

4 Reach up high with your racket. Aim to hit the ball just as it is beginning to fall. Keep your arm, elbow, and wrist loose as you swing. Flick your wrist to add power to your serve.

5 As you follow through, your racket arm will end up around your waist. To keep your balance, bend at the waist and bring your back leg around, then get ready to make your next shot.

Because the serve can be such a powerful shot, serving gives you the edge over your opponent in a game. But there are a few rules you need to learn before you can serve in a match.

Serve rules

The serve is the first shot of every point you play— so it's very important. Play begins when either you or your opponent hits the first serve. The server continues to serve until a player has won the game. Then the non-server takes over. (In doubles, the four players take turns serving.) The serve alternates with games between players until the end of the match (except in a tiebreaker). The server gets two chances to serve for each point.

Serve or return?
To decide who serves first, one player spins a racket and the other guesses which side it will fall on. The winner chooses which end to play or whether to serve. We always choose to serve—it gives us the chance to take control of the match from the first ball. If the winner of the racket spin chooses to serve, the other player decides which end of the court they want to receive. If the winner of the spin chooses which end to play, the other player decides whether to serve or receive. Players swap ends after the first game. For the rest of the set, they change ends after every other game.

Get ready, get set
The serve is taken from behind the baseline. You can line up anywhere between the center mark and the singles sideline on the court. For doubles, most players stand closer to the singles line. In singles, most players stand closer to the center mark, so that they can cover the maximum court space quickly when the serve is returned.

If your opponent can't get their racket anywhere near your serve, let alone return it, your serve is called an ace!

server

The server is ready to serve into the deuce box.

center mark

ad service box

deuce service box

Serve order

Your serve must travel diagonally over the net and bounce into your opponent's service box. The first serve of each game must be hit into the left-hand (or deuce) service box as you look at it across the net. For the second point, you serve into the right-hand (advantage or ad) service box and then alternate between the two. You have two chances to serve into the box for each point. If you miss them both, it's a double fault, and your opponent wins the point.

Tiebreaker

In a tiebreaker, the player who received in the last game serves the first point into the deuce service box. The other player then serves the next two points, hitting the first point to the ad box. After that, the players serve two points alternately until someone wins. Players usually play a 12-point tiebreaker and the first to 7 points wins.

Serve tactics and faults

When you first start to serve, the most important thing is to make sure you hit the ball into play and avoid serving a fault. Otherwise, you'll lose the point without your opponent even hitting a shot! As you gain confidence, you can try to aim the ball at different areas of the box to make it difficult for your opponent to return, but fault-free serving should come before tactics every time!

Tactical serving

If you aim for the top left or right corner of the service box, your opponent will have to scramble to get to the ball. Shoot for the top middle of the box, and the ball will go toward your opponent's body—which makes it difficult to return. If your opponent has a weakness, such as a poor backhand or a floppy forehand, serve to their weaker side. But remember to mix up your serve, or they'll be able to predict where you are going to hit it.

Faulty footwork

It's forbidden to put any part of your foot on the baseline or inside the court before you hit the ball. If you do, it's a foot fault. This is a really annoying way to lose a point and can affect the outcome. So watch out!

Let serve

If a serve hits the top of the net or the net post and then lands inside the service box, it is called a let serve. A let is not a fault—you have a chance to serve again, whether the let serve was your first or second try.

Outside the box

It is a fault to serve a ball that lands outside the lines of the correct service box. If the ball nicks the net and then lands outside the lines, that's also a fault. Second serves are often slower to make sure the ball lands in the box.

Service drill
This drill is a great way to improve the accuracy of your serve. Place groups of three tennis balls, evenly spaced, just inside the service box. Then serve directly at each group, aiming to hit the balls. Your goal is to be able to put the ball in any part of the service box you want to.

Who's at fault?
In a match with a friend, there's no umpire or line judge to call faults. You'll have to do it yourselves. This isn't always easy—many faults are pretty tough calls. Our advice is to be fair and be firm.

Other common faults
As well as missing the service box or foot faulting, there are several other ways you might serve a fault. Remember, any of these on first and second serve will lose you the point.

Serving from a position not in the rules.

Missing the ball as you swing.

Serving a ball that doesn't make it over the net.

39

Returning serve

To win a match, you need to break your opponent's serve. Most young players pay little attention to their return strategy, but you've got to develop reliable return skills to keep the ball in play. Every time you miss a return, you give a free point to your opponent. It's important to make them work for every point on their serve!

Where do you stand?

There is no single best place to be when a serve comes your way, because you can't know what kind of ball your opponent will serve. Start by standing a little behind the baseline. You'll be in the right place to return a hard serve. If you need to rush up for a short serve, it's much easier to run forward than backward.

Stand in the ready position with your feet shoulder-width apart and your knees slightly bent.

Return strategy

You should have a plan based on what you think your opponent is likely to do. For example, if they like coming to the net, hit the return low—below their waist or at their feet. If they stay at the baseline, return the shot higher and deeper. Also aim to hit to your opponent's weaker side. So if the backhand is their weaker shot, hit to that side.

You can usually move into the net a little to receive a second serve.

Go after the return

A slow serve gives you time to "load up" and take a full swing at the ball. Move into the ball, hit it early, and whip it across the net—make your opponent scared to ever hit a soft serve to you again!

Feel the power

If the serve is fast, there won't be time for a large take-back. Shorten your backswing and use the pace of the ball rather than trying to make your own.

41

The basic skills of tennis are so important to master that we think it is worth taking another look at them. Here we give some advice on how to improve aspects of your game.

Basic skills in action

No matter what level your game is at right now, you can play better tennis by focusing on a few fundamental skills. Every player—and that includes both of us—can pull their game up and sharpen their strokes by putting these skills into play. If you're dedicated to being the best you can be, here's how to raise the level of your game.

Footwork
If you hit a blistering forehand, it's your feet and legs that got you into position to make the shot. Footwork gets you to the right place at the right speed and the right time. Get in the habit of moving every time you play.

Agility
To reach a crosscourt ball, you're going to have to run. To hit a low volley, you're going to have to get down to the ball. To hit a smash, you're going to have to leap as high as you can. All these shots, and most others, require agility (quick and easy movement). Doing special exercises will help to improve your agility.

Reaction times
In today's game, especially on a fast surface like grass, it's essential to be able to react instantly to whatever your opponent throws at you. Reaction times will improve with training exercises and match practice. Your actions should become automatic—so you don't have to even think about them. Mental alertness and concentration are vital.

You've got to keep your eyes on the ball every second it is in play. If you look away for even a moment, you will probably lose the point.

Hand–eye coordination

Being able to hit the ball with your racket—which involves judging distance, speed, and height—depends on hand–eye coordination. This will improve the more you play the sport, but it is worth doing throwing-and-catching exercises to develop this vital skill.

Balance

If you lose your balance, it's much more likely you will make an error and lose the point. Keep control of your body at all times and avoid uneven, jerky movements. Stay low when you move. Get into the habit of standing with your feet wide apart to stabilize your balance. Above all, keep your head still. You'll be able to see exactly what's going on.

Ready position

Make taking this position a habit after each shot and before the next one. Bend your knees slightly, feet shoulder-width apart and toes ready to push you off in any direction. Hold the racket up in a central position, so that you can take it back to either side. Keep your head up.

Stepping it up

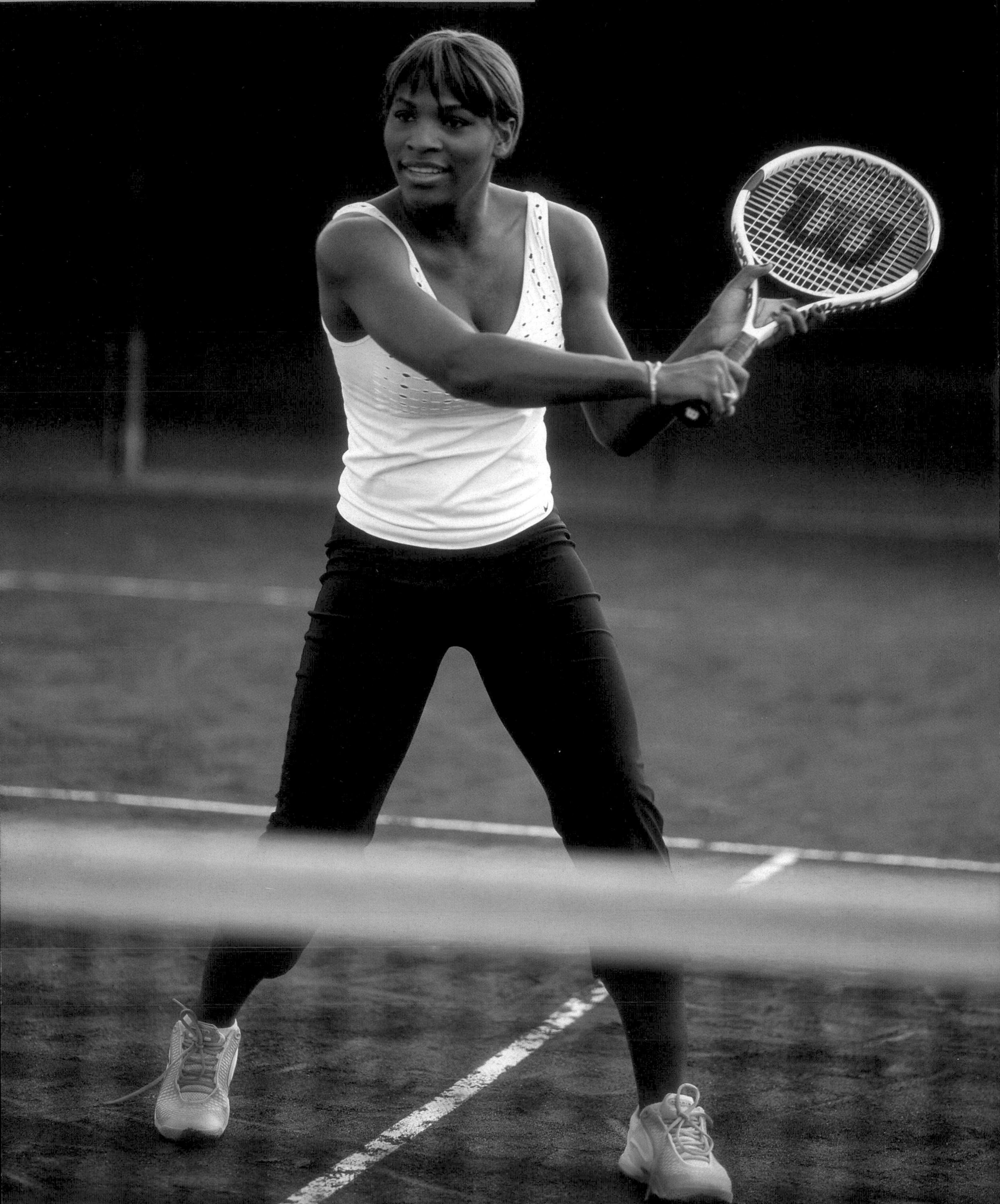

Forehand volley

The forehand volley is a stroke that packs a punch, just what you need to be a "knockout" on court! Hitting a volley doesn't appear to take much effort— there's no big take-back or huge follow-through— but it's vital if you want a great net game. A volley is played before the ball bounces, from a position very close to the net. It's a bold move that piles on the pressure and puts you in charge of the game.

The plot behind the shot

Learning how to volley takes discipline. At first, it's hard to resist bringing your racket back as the ball approaches. Remember that hitting a volley is more like catching the ball than swinging at it. You've got to stop the ball in its path and aim for placement and control.

Forehand volley | **Practice this sequence using your regular forehand grip. As you get better, try the continental grip. This will enable you to hit forehand or backhand volleys without changing your grip at all.**

1 Get ready to attack. Stand about 3 feet (1 meter) from the net with your knees bent and feet shoulder-width apart. Gently cradle the throat of the racket as you hold it in front of you. Stay on your toes.

2 Punch the racket forward to meet the ball in front of your body. Try to hit the ball square on. Keep your grip firm and give the racket handle an extra squeeze as you make contact to add a little more zip.

3 The punching action will create all the follow-through you need. Freeze the racket face in the angle and direction you have volleyed to help direct your shot. Then get ready to move—you've got a lot of ground to cover!

Keep your eyes on the ball so you know when to make contact.

High volley

Reach up for a high volley with everything you've got. Turn your shoulders slightly as you punch through the ball. As the ball leaves the racket face, stop your racket arm or you risk dragging the ball right down into the net.

Use your free arm to help you balance. Lean into the shot with your upper body.

Low volley

Volleying a ball that is lower than the top of the net is extra-tough. Bend down deeply as you step into the ball. Keep the racket face way open to give your volley lift. Don't worry about power—just concentrate on getting that ball up and over the net, deep into your opponent's side of the court.

Open face

Backhand volley

The backhand volley is a crucial part of your net game. Like the forehand volley, it's a stroke that calls for lightning-fast reflexes, strong wrists, and solid footwork. But you can prepare for a backhand volley in a flash, giving you a rapid-fire return that can knock the socks off your opponent. Just remember to keep the racket out in front, move into the ball, and punch it like you mean it.

Threat at the net

The backhand volley is played before the ball bounces, between 3 and 7 feet (1 and 2 meters) from the net; if you are any farther back, it's harder to put one past your opponent. It takes confidence to volley, because net play is all action, all the time.

Backhand volley | We started out with two-handed backhand volleys. After playing a while, we changed to a one-handed grip. This is a tough shot to master in the beginning. Keep at it!

1 As the ball approaches on your backhand side, take your racket back slightly as your upper body turns. Your weight should be on your toes. Step into the ball to meet it and release the racket from your supporting hand.

2 Make contact with the ball in front of your body. Push the racket forward with a short, sharp punch. Keep the racket head above your wrist. Use your free arm to help you balance—and recover quickly.

3 Keep your follow-through short and sweet. Drive the racket through the point of contact. Almost as soon as the ball leaves the strings, hold your racket still for a moment. You could face a fast return, and you'll need to get ready.

Backhand volley

When you hit the ball in front of your body, you can keep an eye on it at all times.

Keep your grip firm and steady as you take a short jab at the ball.

Way up high

The high backhand volley is a tough shot. When you see a high ball on its way, position yourself so you will be behind it when you strike. Aim to hit the ball deep, but if you have to, just block it back to your opponent.

Way down low

Low backhand volleys are tricky. It's not easy to get the ball up and over the net and still keep it in court. When you spot a low ball, get down to meet it. Turn your upper body sideways as you take the racket back, and crouch down with your weight on the back foot. Step forward to meet the ball, and punch under and up through the ball. Tilt the racket face a little to give the ball enough lift to sail over the net.

The **lob**

Look, up in the sky! Is it a bird, a plane—or a lob? Whether it's a forehand or a backhand, a lob is a shot hit high up in the air. You want to lift that ball right over your opponent's racket. The lob may not be one of the foundations of your game, but it is a handy little shot that can help you stay in the point.

To lob or not to lob?

A lob is useful in a number of situations. You can use it to buy a little time when your opponent catches you off guard and you can't get in position for a groundstroke. You can also lob a shot over an opponent who has come close to the net for a volley. Just remember that your lob should be high, otherwise you may provide your opponent with an opportunity to smash the ball back over the net. Try to lob to your opponent's backhand side—backhand smashes are very difficult to hit!

| The lob | Practice this sequence to help you to get to grips with the lob. It's a useful shot to master, since an unexpected lob is a great way to change the pace of a game. |

1 Hold your racket with the same grip you use for your forehand drive. As soon as the ball comes your way, put your non-racket arm out for balance. Turn your shoulders and take the racket back low.

2 Step into the ball as it falls. If the ball is low, you can make yourself lower by bending your knees. Swing your racket forward in an upward path. Your racket arm should be slightly bent.

3 Keep your head still with your eyes on the ball. Try to make contact with the ball to the side and slightly in front of your body. The racket head should be level, and the racket face should be open so you get the best lift.

Lob? What lob?

Once you've mastered the lob, the next thing you should do is learn how to hide it! It makes sense—if you've developed a secret weapon, you don't want your opponent to see it coming. Try disguising your lob by using your typical groundstroke backswing. Very crafty!

Backhand lob

Use a backhand lob to scoop up a ball on your backhand side. The basics are the same as for a forehand lob: use the same grip you use for a groundstroke, get down low, and follow up high.

4 Finish the shot by bringing your racket way up, across your body and over your shoulder. The better your follow-through, the better your lob. Get back into position to prepare for your next shot.

The **overhead smash**

The overhead smash is the ultimate power shot, but it also takes a lot of concentration. You need great aim and perfect timing for a successful shot. If you've got the confidence and control to get it right, your opponent is unlikely to be able to return your smash, and you'll almost certainly win the point.

Up and over

The overhead smash can be hit from both forehand and backhand sides. You'll get the power of your entire body behind it, slamming the ball deep into the dusty corners of your opponent's court. An overhead smash is often used in response to a lob shot.

1 Stand sideways-on to the court. Your feet should be apart and your knees slightly bent. Bend your elbow as you start to take your racket up. Point to the ball with your other hand as you get into position.

2 Use the same "throwing" motion that you use when you serve. Take your racket back behind your shoulder, keeping your elbow up high. Push up with your back leg and turn your shoulders into the shot.

3 Aim to hit the ball when it's in front of your body and when your arm is fully extended. Flick your wrist forward and down as you make contact. This will aim the ball in the direction you want it to go.

As you bring the racket head down, be careful not to drag the ball down into the net!

Quick thinking

As soon as you spot a lob coming your way, think fast—and move even faster. Can you let the ball bounce first, which will make your shot easier? Or is the ball at the right level for an airborne shot? Either way, make up your mind and move. Sidestep so you keep your balance. You want the ball to be above and in front of your body.

It can be hard to work out where the falling ball will come down. Try pointing at the ball to help you keep your eyes locked on it.

4 Bring your racket head down through the ball. Turn your body back toward your opponent and adjust your feet to help you keep your balance. Bring your racket foot forward to stop the forward momentum of your body.

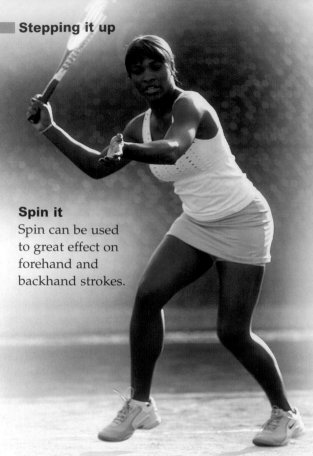

Spin it
Spin can be used to great effect on forehand and backhand strokes.

Slice and topspin

Once you are confident with your basic strokes, it's time to put a new spin on them. Because a ball hit with slice or spin travels differently, it can catch your opponent off guard. Learning how to add spin takes practice, but before long it will come naturally.

Why slice or spin?

Hitting a ball with a bit of spin (slice or topspin) mixed in helps your game in two big ways. First, spin enables you to really control the ball. You can alter both its flight path and its speed, so the ball goes exactly where you want it to go. Second, using spin tactically can throw your opponent off their game. Sneak in some spin—forehand or backhand—and you can wreak havoc with the rhythm of your opponent's game. Slice and topspin also add variety to your serve.

Backhand slice | The one-handed sliced backhand is a useful stroke. You can use it to mix things up or if you find yourself out of position on court.

1 The sliced backhand is a vital stroke to master. A sliced ball has backspin. This means it rotates backward while traveling forward through the air. It lands low, so it's tough to return. Before hitting the shot, stand in the ready position.

2 Take back the racket as usual, but at the end of the take-back, raise the racket head a little above the level you intend to strike. Keep the racket face slightly open (angled up). You want to cut from behind the ball, hitting from high to low, so the ball will skim the net.

3 As you step into your shot, slide the racket face under the ball. It should feel like you are serving it up on a platter. The racket face should be open, at an angle of about 45 degrees. Make contact with the ball slightly ahead of your body. Balance with your non-hitting arm.

What is topspin?

A ball hit with topspin spins toward your opponent. It falls to the court quickly, and when it bounces, it kicks up high, making it difficult to hit.

The slice is a useful shot to pull out when you are approaching the net or when you want to change the pace of a rally to your advantage.

Topspin

To add topspin, you use a closed racket face—the racket face is angled down and slightly toward the ground. Take the racket back, but just as you feel you are about to put your weight into the strike, drop the racket head into a lower position. Then swing the racket upward at impact, brushing against the back of the ball. The faster the racket moves, the more spin you get.

4 After you hit the ball, your racket arm is extended out to the front and the racket is taken forward and down. The racket face is open. The follow-through can be a short chop, or you can lift the racket to about head height. The follow-through is what sends the ball forward.

5 When a sliced ball lands, it bounces low, forcing your opponent to dig deep. You've got to hit the ball with confidence, though. A weak slice seems to move so slowly over the net, you feel like your opponent can read the writing on the ball before it arrives!

The **drop shot**

Sometimes you only need a whisper to make your point. The drop shot is hit to barely clear the net before landing just over it. It's the softest shot in the game—but one of the hardest to return! You'll have your opponent scrambling to the ball with little chance of reaching it. The drop shot is not easy to master, but if you can pull it off when the time is right, the point is yours.

Drop in

If your opponent is back behind the baseline or off to one side of the court, a drop shot can catch them out. You can also use the shot to force them to the net—useful if their net game is weak or if you are planning a killer lob.

Forehand drop shot | **You need to be ready with your drop shot whenever the opportunity presents itself. Use these steps to practice until you have total confidence in your shot.**

1 Take your racket back higher than you would for a volley. Start to bring it forward, leading with the bottom edge. Direct your swing along a slightly downward path. Bend your knees a little.

2 Just before you make contact, turn your racket face so that it is open. It should almost face the sky. Cut up and through the very bottom of the ball with a slicing motion. Don't clobber it—caress it!

3 Let your racket follow through to nudge the ball over the net. Your follow-through should be short enough to take speed off the ball, but not so short that you lose backspin.

When racket meets ball

The way you make contact is the secret to a deadly drop shot. Imagine that you are catching the ball on your racket. Scrape the strings down the back of the ball for spin, then use your wrist to scoop the ball up and over the net.

Never try a drop shot if you are behind the baseline—the ball might not clear the net! You should be closer to the service line than the baseline.

To play a drop shot, use your usual groundstroke grip or try a continental grip to add a bit of slice.

Backhand drop

Many players find slicing feels more natural from the backhand side. It is also easier to disguise a backhand drop shot. Cut down behind the ball and lift it just over the net.

57

Tennis **etiquette**

Not all of the rules in tennis are written down. But the unwritten practices and customs that make up on-court etiquette are just as important to the game. Tennis is a very competitive sport, and when things get intense, it's easy to lose control of your behavior. But try hard not to. You've got to show respect for your opponent, yourself, and the rules of the game. So, play nice!

Before you play

Good sportsmanship begins before the first ball is hit. If you arrange to play a match with someone, make sure you arrive about 15 minutes early. Bring along a can of balls. It's normal to exchange shots for about five minutes to warm up before you start playing. (This also gives you a chance to spot your opponent's weaknesses!)

Tennis etiquette | The unwritten rules of tennis are very important. Here are some guidelines that you should try to follow whenever you are on court.

Ball etiquette

You are in charge of collecting the balls on your side of the net. (Of course, if you hit one into the middle of nowhere, you should be the one to go and find it, even if it's not on your side.) If you hit a ball into another court, wait until the point is over before you ask for your ball back.

Getting balls to the server

You should make sure that the player who serves always has two balls before starting a point. If the first serve is a fault, you can let the ball go by, catch it and pocket it, or return it very gently. Or send the ball to the net or the back fence, where it won't be in the way.

Calling the lines

Each player is responsible for calling the balls in or out on their side of the court. It can be hard, but try to judge questionable shots as well as you can and trust your opponent to do the same. Make the call quickly and decisively. If you can't agree, play the point again.

What's the score?

The server is in charge of keeping score and must call it out at the end of each point. If you disagree with the score, politely ask your opponent to go over recent events in the game with you. If you can't agree, find a point you do agree on and play from there.

Tennis is a competitive game, and naturally you will be happy to win a point or a match. But have some respect for your opponent and don't go overboard with your celebrations.

Bad behavior
Cursing, throwing your racket around, deliberately stalling for time, or venting your anger all take your mind off the matter at hand—the game. We all get frustrated sometimes, but it's important not to lose control. Take a deep breath and calm yourself down before you do something you'll regret!

After the match
Whether we've won or lost, we always respect our opponent after the last ball is played. We shake hands and say, "Good match!" A few friendly words can go a long way.

Keeping cool and polite under pressure is important not only in tennis but in everyday life!

Playing at the **baseline**

The baseline is the battleground where you'll fight for most of your points. And believe us: when you stand at the back of the court, ready to rock, you'll see just how much ground you've got to cover. Lots of players tend to stay well behind the baseline when they're just starting out, playing a defensive game. But as you gain in confidence, you can move right up to the baseline and hit attacking shots that will have your opponent on the run!

Decisions, decisions

Of course, you're going to need an arsenal of groundstrokes to fight a baseline battle. But it's your tactical skills that will really give you the winning edge. You need to decide how to handle every ball that comes your way. The more you practice and play, the faster you'll be able to make good decisions.

Getting started

To build your baseline game, you need a hitting partner. Each of you should take a ready position on the baseline. Begin to hit the ball back and forth. Try to hit the ball right to each other and agree on either forehands or backhands. Once you feel confident that you can return the ball consistently, start to mix up the shots, hitting to both to the forehand and backhand side. Make sure you move into the ready position between shots.

Two's company

Another way of honing your baseline rallying skills is to practice against two players. A popular drill requires that you hit your forehands and backhands crosscourt while the net players volley down the line. This forces you to cover the baseline at all times and means that you are constantly switching between forehand and backhand shots. Soon you will not have to think about what shot to choose; it will just come automatically. Aim your groundstrokes at your hitting partners to develop control and consistency.

We like to play an aggressive baseline game to win each point. But we will move toward the net if our opponent hits a weak shot.

Mixing it up

With practice, you'll feel at ease with choosing your stroke, moving to the ball, and giving it your best shot. Practice is a great time to develop your decision-making skills about how to play each ball. By directing your shots down the line and crosscourt, you will keep your opponent on the run. Your deep groundstrokes will often force your opponent to hit short balls. Make sure you take advantage of the short response by hitting a good approach shot (*see* page 64) and following it into the net.

Place your shots

We always have a plan of where we want the ball to go before we hit it. Place your shots carefully. Use crosscourt shots to set up your opponent. Try hitting a shot down the sideline (called "down the line") to end the point. Aim the ball at a point of no return.

Topspin will help you control the ball and keep it in the court.

Down-the-line shots are consistent point winners because they have less distance to travel.

Remember your footwork: the open-stance forehand is extremely popular with advanced players.

You need quick reactions and confidence to play well at the net.

Coming into **the net**

Lots of players who are just starting out won't go near the net, except to shake hands! But if you want to win matches, you'll need to be comfortable anywhere on court—including at the net. Taking position at the net is a bold move that immediately shows your opponent you mean business. Follow our advice to develop your net game, and you'll soon be on top.

Choose your moment
You can't simply stroll up to the net and volley—you've got to choose your moment. If your opponent hits a ball that falls short, you've just been handed a one-way ticket to the net. Otherwise, you will have to set up the situation yourself with a solid approach shot (*see* below). Take an explosive first step into the net and use the split-step as your opponent plays the ball.

Serve and volley
If you want to cause trouble when your opponent is returning service, you can charge the net after your serve. Toss the ball slightly in front of you so that your body is always drawn forward and aim down the middle of the service box. (A wide serve could be angled back to pass you.) Move toward the net after you serve and get into position, with knees bent and racket ready as your opponent returns the ball.

Approach and volley
Coming to the net to volley really turns up the heat on court. Begin your attack when returning a short ball. Fire off an approach shot—the stroke played before you move into volley position. Try to take the ball early and on the rise, so your opponent has less time to prepare. Aim the ball as deep and low as you can (if hitting a slice approach), preferably to their weaker side. Forcing your opponent back to the baseline puts them on the defensive.

Standing at the net will often intimidate your opponent, making them miss their next shot.

No contact!

When playing at the net, it is vital that you do not touch it with any part of your body, racket, or clothing, including your shoes. If you do so while the ball is in play, you will lose the point. You're not allowed to reach over the net to play the ball either, unless wind or spin causes the ball to bounce on your side and then go back over the net before bouncing again. It sounds unlikely but it does sometimes happen!

Playing at **the net**

Being at the net gives you a good chance of winning the point, but things can go wrong. One moment, you could be towering near the net, dominating the point. The next, you could be watching the ball sail right by you! Here is the lowdown on playing— attacking and defending—at the net.

Always stay alert when playing at the net. A volley may come at you from any direction and require you to reach, jump, or get down low.

Volleying

The volley (*see* pages 46–49) is the key to your net game. Because you are so close to the net when you volley, it's easy to direct this punchy little shot. You can usually give the ball enough pace and angle to get it beyond your opponent's reach.

Cover the court

Closing in on the net can be a risky business. If you can't put the ball away for a clean point, your position near the net makes you extremely vulnerable to a lob, a passing shot down either sideline, or a ball hit straight at you. Keep a strong, central court position and be on your toes at all times.

Entice into the net

If your opponent has a weak volley or tends to avoid the net altogether, try to force them to move forward with a series of short balls. They'll be uncomfortable at the net, and the speedy pace of net play might fluster them into making mistakes, allowing you to pounce on the point.

Beating a net player

Your first defense against a net attack is the passing shot. You simply hit the ball to an area of the court that your opponent can't reach. If a passing shot fails, a good lob will get them scrambling back to the baseline.

When hitting a low volley at the net, it is vital to get down to the ball by bending your knees.

Volley drill

Practice this drill to improve your net play. Stand near the net with your non-racket arm behind your back. As your coach hits balls to you, return them with backhand and forehand volleys. Focus on keeping the racket head up.

Fast forward

The action at the net is intense. It feels like there are twice as many things to think about in half the time. You'll have to react fast. Use short steps and always be ready to move. When you volley, keep the action short and sharp.

Match tips

Anyone who's ever played tennis knows that it can be a very competitive game. Every player is on the lookout for that certain something that will give them a little extra edge. Just what that "something" is may be hard to define, because there's no single technique or skill that will put you ahead of the rest. Follow our advice, though, and you'll be well prepared when you step out on court.

A short practice right before a match helps you be sharp and ready for the challenge. Don't overdo it, though, or you'll tire yourself out!

Have confidence in yourself
The more you play, the more you will come to understand your own game. Believe in yourself. Even if you are thoroughly beaten, try to learn something from the match that will help improve your game.

Heads up

Your performance during a match is both emotional and physical, and your mental attitude can make or break your game. Each match will bring new challenges, and you will need to confront them. Prepare yourself mentally before you take your position on court.

Check out your opposition

Familiarize yourself with your opponent before you get on court. Talk to others who have played them. Think about what you're likely to face from your opponent and figure out how you should react. It will be easier to anticipate shots and work up a game plan if you have a good idea of what's coming.

Chilling out

A good warm-up is crucial, especially if you're playing in cold conditions. If it's cold, you should layer your clothing and remove the top layers as you start to heat up. Remember—balls and strings can also get cold and may lose a bit of zing, so you'll need to adjust your strokes accordingly.

Have fun

The most important thing in tennis is to enjoy yourself. Playing should be about having fun out there, even if it's a tough match. You have to have a sense of humor and keep things in perspective.

Fun in the sun

The sun's glare can sometimes make the ball nearly impossible to see. If you're facing the sun, block it with a visor or cap and sunglasses and use your non-racket hand to shade your eyes on high balls. Protect your skin with sunblock and reapply frequently. Hydrate yourself with lots of water and sports drinks.

69

Match tactics

The match is on: are you ready to strike? There is plenty you can do to get ready before the first ball is served. Once play begins, trust in your game. Stay with what works, but don't be afraid to raise the stakes from time to time. Put 100 percent into every shot, and you will likely be the winner.

Ball placement

Controlling both the direction and depth of each ball you hit will give you a definite match advantage. Hitting the ball from side to side or varying the depth keeps your opponent on the run, wearing them down. You can also direct balls to their weak spot. Taking a little pace off the ball—or picking up the pace—messes with your opponent's timing and can draw them into making errors.

Consistency

Being consistent doesn't mean playing like a boring ball machine. It's all about choosing the best shot at the right time and hitting that shot as well as you can. It's great when you pull an amazing shot out of nowhere to end the point, but it's even more important to hit the ball consistently over the net.

Get a move on

Split-step, slide, shuffle, or sprint—whatever you do, just get to the ball! If the ball is coming right toward you, and you have a choice between a forehand or backhand return, play to your strength. If your backhand is weaker, run around the ball in a tight C-shaped path and launch a forehand stroke.

Stay in the point

Don't take huge risks to win. Smart shots are often better than spectacular shots. Do what it takes to keep yourself in the point. If you've been cornered, get the ball back deep down the middle or across the court. Send up a lob, if need be. The more shots you get in, the better your chances of winning the point.

Go for it

Of course, the most important thing is keeping the ball in play. But if you see an opportunity to be bold, and you are fairly sure you can nail it, let go. Be aggressive. If you lose the point, at least you will know that you have given it your all.

If you lose a point, try to put it out of your mind right away so you can concentrate on winning the next point. Never give up, no matter how far down you are.

Use the whole court

It's not always enough to simply power the ball past your opponent. It's a big court, so try to work every bit of it to gain control of the match. Come to the net whenever you can, cover all the angles, and open up gaps on your opponent's court to give yourself as many opportunities as possible.

Making mistakes

Everyone makes mistakes during a match—including us. And when you've slipped up once, it's easy to tumble down the slippery slope of making multiple errors. It is crucial not to panic and let your game slide. As tough as it may seem, try to put errors behind you and move on. Look at them as chances to start again and show your best stuff.

Playing **doubles**

The game of doubles shares the same basic rules and scoring system as singles, and players use the same strokes. But in other ways, it's a whole new ball game. You'll need to be especially accurate with your shots because there are two people ready to jump on them. You'll also need to tune up your reflexes, since the pace of the game can be lightning fast. The skills you develop playing doubles will definitely help your singles game.

Doubles court

The alleys are used in doubles tennis—the outer sidelines mark the side edges of the court (*see* page 14). This bigger court gives you more space to play, but since there are two of you at each end, there is less court for each player to cover. Teams flip a coin or spin a racket to win their choice of serving first or picking the end. If one team chooses to serve first, the other decides which end of the court they will play at the start of the match.

Serving rules

Players must agree on a serving rotation before the match and stick to it. If a team has chosen to serve first, one player serves the opening game, and the other serves the third game in the set. On the other side of the net, one player serves the second game, and the other serves the fourth game. You must also decide which player is going to receive service first and on what side of the court they are going to stand.

Cover the court

You and your partner should have the middle of the court covered. By doing this, you will force your opponents to hit wide shots and increase the chance that they will hit the ball out of court.

It can take time to get used to playing with a partner. Practice makes perfect!

Doubles rules

A doubles match has more or less the same rules as a singles match. One important rule for doubles is that, although there are two players on each side, only one player from each team may hit each shot. If the ball is touched a second time, the point goes to the other team.

Service position

When serving in doubles, stand at the baseline, a little closer to the sidelines than your singles service spot. Your partner should stand in the service box, about halfway between the service line and the net. If the player is too close to the net, the ball could zing past before there is time for them to time to react.

Returning the serve

When it's your team's turn to return the serve, use a similar one-up, one-back formation. The player returning the serve should stand just behind the baseline in a central position. The other player should stand on the service line, between the center line and the sideline.

Here we are playing doubles in the 2000 Olympic Games.

Doubles talk

Playing a great doubles game demands real teamwork. A winning doubles team seems to move as one as they cover the court—and cover for each other. Good communication both before and during the match is key. You need to make sure your partner always knows what your next move will be. After you play with the same partner for a while, anticipating each other's moves will come naturally.

Perfect partners

We're lucky—we have each other. If you're looking for a doubles partner, however, look for someone with excellent communication skills. These are essential for helping you develop your best possible doubles game. Find a person whose attitude to the game matches yours, and someone whose strengths and weaknesses balance yours.

Talking tactics

You and your partner are a team, so you've got to communicate well. We've played together so many times that we know each other's games like our own. That's what you and your partner should aim for. Before a match, decide on your tactics, so you're both clear on how you are going to play.

Teamwork

As you play, talk to each other between points. Encourage your partner to do their best, and if they make a great shot, let them know you're happy. If things aren't going so well, talk about how you could adapt your strategy. It's okay to be constructive, but not critical. Remember, there's no "I" in teamwork!

Hand signals

Some doubles teams use hand signals to communicate secretly (although hand signals are not often used at professional level). The player closest to the net puts a hand behind their back to signal to the server. Signals can tell your partner where to serve or let them know what you're planning to do.

It is normal in doubles teams for one player to always play on the left and the other on the right. The choice depends on each player's strengths and weaknesses.

Try these signals or make some up for yourselves—just make sure you both remember what they mean!

Here are some hand signals and what they usually mean:

1 Open hand—"I will intercept"
2 Clenched fist—"I will stay on my side"
3 Finger pointing sideways—"serve wide"

Doubles strategy

If you and your partner want to pose a double threat on court, you'll need to put both your heads together and think tactics. Because it's crowded out there with four people on court, some of the strategies you use in your singles game aren't going to work in doubles. But one key factor remains the same: if you want to win, you'll have to take control of the net.

Attack the ball

When you serve, your teammate stands in an attacking position close to the net, ready to pounce on the return of serve if it comes their way.

Service strategy

Try to serve deep to the receiver's weakness so you can prepare to attack. In doubles, it's extra- important to make your first serve a good one. The return of serve player usually will aim crosscourt to avoid their partner at the net. A good tactic is to have your opponent poach (*see* page 77) on the return to keep your opponents off balance.

Doubles is an exciting game to play and watch because it is so fast. Playing doubles is also a chance to share your skills and get the best out of your partner.

Dynamic duo

Remember, even the cleverest tactics won't work without teamwork. You and your partner need to think together, move together, and play together to achieve your very best doubles game. That's what we try to do when we play together.

Take aim

Directing your shots is especially important to your doubles game, since there are two players ready to return each shot. Your best chance is to aim your shots under, over, or between your opponents. If they are charging the net, for example, try to aim the ball at their feet—it's tough to "scoop up" a ball down by your shoestrings.

Get to the net

Try to control play at the net. The mere presence of a player stalking close to the net can be intimidating to the other team. So why not double up the fear factor? After you've served, try moving forward to get into a good volleying position. At the net, keep an equal distance away from your partner and move together, whether forward, backward, or sideways.

Poaching

Once you're comfortable at the net, you can pick off balls that aren't returned at enough of an angle or with enough speed and send them straight back. This move is called poaching, and it's one of the key tactics in good doubles play. Poaching is most common when the net player jumps on a weak service return.

Keeping fit for life

There are days when we never pick up a tennis racket. But we do fit in some kind of physical activity every day. Whether it's walking our dogs, surfing, or skateboarding, regular exercise is important for fitness and health. Taking good care of your body pays off big time when you play. You can also target workouts to benefit your tennis game. Go on, get it moving!

Jogging is a great way to keep fit and can really help improve your stamina, which is so important in tennis.

Mixing it up
Don't stick with just one sport or exercise routine. Working out shouldn't feel like work. Try a variety of activities to improve your overall athletic skills. Focus on building stamina, flexibility, and strength, and your tennis game will reap the benefits.

Strengthening exercises
Most tennis strokes start with turning your shoulders and body, so it helps to strengthen your oblique (side) muscles. Try sitting back-to-back with a partner and passing the ball around you. Change direction after each set.

Jumping rope is a really good cardiovascular exercise and is great for conditioning your body. Wear supportive footwear, since you'll be doing lots of bouncing!

To work your shoulders and upper arms, stand facing a partner and toss a weighted ball back and forth. Try to build up to three sets of 10 to 15 repetitions.

This exercise works the muscles that help you rotate your body.

On the ball

Using an exercise ball for strength training helps isolate the muscles you want to work and reduces the strain on your lower back. Crunches that firm up your tummy and work the back muscles are especially effective with the ball.

Lie with your stomach against the ball, legs slightly bent. Stretch your elbows out and place your fingertips at the sides of your head. Lift your upper body and legs at the same time, and hold.

Try to maintain your hold for one to five seconds. Release slowly, and gently return to your starting position. Repeat the stretch, working up to three sets of 10 to 15 repetitions.

Working with weights

If you want to put some real power behind your strokes, use free weights to target specific muscles. Stick with lighter weights (one-, three-, and five-pound weights) to add power without bulk. Too many muscles will cut down on your speed. Check with your family doctor before beginning a weight-training program.

This exercise develops and shapes the deltoid muscles at the front of your arm. Stand with a light weight in each hand and slowly extend one arm until it is parallel to the floor. Repeat with the other arm.

Lunges with weights work the quadriceps (thigh) muscles. Stand with a light weight in each hand, arms at your sides. Step forward with your right foot, bending your left knee as you move. Bring your leg back and repeat for three sets of 10 to 15 repetitions, then do three sets leading with your left leg.

Preparing for a match

There's no doubt about it, walking out on court for your first big match is scary. It might seem like the net is twice as high as it was yesterday, and that the court itself has doubled in size. We'll help you banish the butterflies and prepare to do your very best. You probably feel like you have a mountain to climb, but if you take it just one point at a time, you'll get to the top. So what if you stumble now and then? Another point will come along soon enough.

A winning attitude

In tennis, somebody's got to win, somebody's got to lose. You may have practiced and prepared for a match like a pro, but sometimes it's not enough, and you lose. Don't let it get you down. You need to stay positive—a winning attitude will help make you a winner.

Before the match

Start your pre-match prep work the night before the match with a good evening meal. Include foods with plenty of unprocessed (complex) carbohydrates: whole-grains, such as brown rice, wholegrain bread, and whole-wheat pasta. These provide your body with energy in the form of glycogen, so loading up on carbs will give you an energy boost when you need it most.

Brown rice **Whole-wheat pasta** **Whole-grain bread**

Pre-match check list:

- two rackets (in case the strings break on one racket)
- a can of balls
- clothes you plan to play in;
  a warm-up jacket and pants; socks and shoes
- a hat or headband and wristbands
- sunblock
- a box of large bandages for blisters
- a few snacks (apples and bananas are great)
- plenty of water and sports drinks
- don't forget to add something that motivates you: your music and headphones, a good book—whatever works for you
- a winning attitude!

Match day

About three hours before you play, eat a meal to help keep your muscles fueled. Again, nibble on complex carbs that will help keep your blood sugar stable. Peanut butter and banana on whole-wheat toast, oatmeal with fresh fruits, or low-fat yogurt with chopped apples and a little brown sugar are great breakfast choices. For lunch, you might choose a sandwich of lean protein like chicken and lots of vegetables on whole-grain bread. Keep hydrating yourself with water or the occasional sports drink.

Good to go

Get yourself courtside with plenty of time to spare. Not only is it rude to keep people waiting, you want to make sure you have time to warm up properly. Some people like to keep to themselves before a match and avoid much contact with others. There are players who prefer not to focus so much, until the match begins. Your own temperament will guide you to what approach is best.

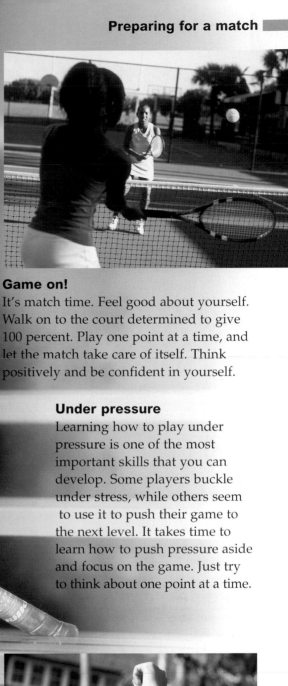

Game on!

It's match time. Feel good about yourself. Walk on to the court determined to give 100 percent. Play one point at a time, and let the match take care of itself. Think positively and be confident in yourself.

Under pressure

Learning how to play under pressure is one of the most important skills that you can develop. Some players buckle under stress, while others seem to use it to push their game to the next level. It takes time to learn how to push pressure aside and focus on the game. Just try to think about one point at a time.

Game over

Whether you win or lose, remember your tennis etiquette and be gracious. A short stretching routine will help you cool down properly. You'll probably be hungry enough to eat your racket. This is a great time for a bagel or some rice cakes, with fresh fruit. This should help your body get some energy back quickly.

Tennis in your life

We make a living from tennis, but it's only just one part of our lives. We've spent countless hours on court, but we've also logged in school time, family time, spiritual time, friend time, and of course, fun time! Tennis isn't everything. If you're hurt, tired, or you've got a big test tomorrow, don't force yourself to play. Whatever your ranking, treat yourself as number one—every day.

You've got to find a balance in your life and hold on to your sense of fun!

Tennis and you

There's a lot to gain from tennis. You'll learn how taking risks (and sometimes failing) is an important part of life, and you'll develop valuable skills. But at the end of the day, it's about enjoying playing tennis.

Group lessons can be fun and affordable. You can learn lots from other players, too!

Before you sign up with a private instructor, meet to discuss fees and to get a feel for the instructor's teaching style.

Tennis lessons

If you're serious about your game, consider tennis lessons. For group lessons, start at your local public court or check with your recreation department to get a schedule of lessons. You can also contact the national or regional branches of a tennis association for a list of programs in your area. If you want one-on-one attention, you'll need private coaching. Look for a teacher who is certified with your national tennis association—ask around at public courts or private clubs for a recommendation.

Remember, there are lots of other things in your life that are important!

Get smart
Maybe all you can think about is hitting a volley, but you'd better hit the books first. Your education should be your number-one priority. If your grades are slipping, stuff your tennis bag under the bed for a while. Once you've pulled things together at school, you'll get back out there.

Don't burn yourself out
Tennis all the time is a recipe for burnout. If you play too much tennis too soon, your brain and body will get tired. Our parents kept us away from competitive tennis for years when we were young, to help us focus on school and reduce pressure. Lots of people didn't agree with them, but they were right. If you're burning out or getting tired of tennis, step back a little and focus on the fun.

The **greatest**

Each time we play at Wimbledon, we remember that Althea Gibson was the first African American to play at this famous championship.

Between us, we've probably been through hundreds of rackets, a million miles of strings, and enough tennis balls to circle the globe! There were times when it was tough, but we always kept on going. Why? Most importantly, our family believed in us from day one, and, of course, they were always there for us, through the highs and the lows. We also draw a lot of inspiration from watching other players, past and present. Seeing others give their all to the game reminds us how much we love to play.

Venus on Serena
She's my kid sister, and my favorite player, ever. Serena's got a powerful forehand, a formidable serve, a big heart, and a barrel of fight! I love playing doubles with her.

Serena on Venus
She's my role model and my best friend. It was inevitable that we would end up facing each other in finals someday—we were both raised to believe we would be champions!

Happy memories | **We've come a long way since we first picked up a racket. Here are a few of our favorite moments!**

Wimbledon
This is an incredibly special place for us because we had dreamed of winning there for so long. Playing each other in the 2002 and 2003 singles finals was a huge thrill. When we play at Wimbledon, particularly on Centre Court, we feel like we are a part of tennis history.

Olympic gold
We'd been champions before, but winning the gold medal in doubles at the 2000 Olympic Games in Sydney, Australia, was the icing on the cake. We treasure our Olympic medals, and we were especially thrilled to win together! Venus also won the gold in the singles competition.

Grand Slam
Nothing compares to winning a Grand Slam. The competition is fierce, and the crowds are just electric. Serena got there first in 1999, winning the U.S. Open singles title, but Venus won Wimbledon a year later. Here we are holding the 2003 Australian Open doubles trophy.

Martina Navratilova

Nobody attacks the ball like Martina. She used her volley to help rack up an incredible 167 singles titles—that's more than any other player, male or female. Her longtime rival, Chris Evert, played a totally different game, but somehow they brought out the very best in each other.

Althea Gibson

A real hero to us both, Althea Gibson overcame incredible odds to show the world she was the greatest. She opened doors not only for women, but also for people of color.

Monica Seles

The only thing tougher than Monica's shots is her must-win attitude. Her astonishing two-handed groundstrokes rarely miss their mark. She plays to win, but she never loses her cool.

Arthur Ashe

An inspiration on and off the court, Arthur Ashe was the first (and only) African American man to win the U.S. Open (1968) and Wimbledon (1975). In spite of personal tragedy, he worked for the good of others, campaigning against inequalities in tennis and the wider world. He was not just a great athlete but a great man.

Pete Sampras

He made it all look so easy, but Pete's game was lethal. There was so much power in every serve and stroke, and he always kept his cool. His serve was in a league of its own.

Glossary

Ace A winning serve that lands out of reach of the receiver.

Ad court The right-hand half of your opponent's court (as you look at it).

Ad service box Your opponent's right-hand service box (as you look at it).

Advantage If the score reaches deuce (40–40), the next player to win a point has the advantage. If they win the next point, they win the game.

Alley The long, narrow rectangle on either side of a tennis court between the singles sideline and the doubles sideline.

Approach shot A groundstroke made when moving to the net.

Backcourt The area behind the baseline.

Backhand A shot played on the left-hand side of your body if you are right-handed and on the right-hand side of your body if you are left-handed.

Backspin *see* **slice**.

Baseline The line along the back boundary of the court.

Beam The area on either side of the racket head.

Center mark The short line that marks the center of the baseline.

Center service line The line that divides the service area into two halves.

Closed racket When the racket head is angled down toward the ground.

Closed stance *see* **square stance**.

Crosscourt A shot played diagonally across the court.

Deuce The score when the players have reached 40–40.

Deuce court The left-hand side of your opponent's court (as you look at it).

Deuce service box Your opponent's left-hand service box (as you look at it).

Double fault When both first and second serves do not land in the correct service box, causing the server to lose the point.

Doubles Tennis between two teams of two players each.

Down the line A shot that sends the ball along or close to the sideline.

Drive A groundstroke that drives the ball deep into the opponent's court.

Drop shot A ball hit very lightly that lands just over the other side of the net, forcing the opponent to rush forward.

Fault A serve that does not go in.

Flat stroke A ball hit without any spin or slice.

Follow-through The continuing movement of the racket after making contact with the ball.

Foot fault If the server's foot hits the baseline or inside the court before they hit the ball, the serve does not count.

Forecourt The area between the net and the service line.

Forehand A shot played on the right-hand side of your body if you are right-handed and on the left-hand side of your body if you are left-handed.

Game A game starts when a new player serves. The game is over when one player (or doubles team) wins four points and is at least two points ahead.

Gauge A measurement of the thickness of a racket string.

Grip The part of the racket at the end of the shaft. Also, the way that a player holds the racket.

Groundstroke A shot played from the backcourt or baseline after the ball has bounced.

Head The area of the racket where the strings are.

Let When a serve clips the net but goes into the correct service box, it is called a let and is replayed. Also, when players decide to replay a point if they are not sure whether a ball is in or out.

Lob A high shot played over an opponent while they are close to the net.

Love A tennis score of zero.

Match A contest in which one player or doubles team tries to beat another player or doubles team over three or five sets of tennis.

Match point The score when a player or doubles team needs just one more point to win a match.

Net ball A ball that touches the net but remains in play.

Open racket When the racket head is angled up toward the sky.

Open stance A position in which the feet and hips point toward the net.

Overhead smash A shot used to hit a high ball with power, often in response to a lob.

Passing shot A shot hit out of the reach of a player who is standing at the net.

Rally A sequence of shots played across the net between players or doubles teams during a point.

Ready hop *see* **split-step**.

Ready position The stance a player takes when ready to receive a ball.

Return The shot that returns the ball to the server or any shot in a rally.

Serve or **service** The shot played by one player from behind the baseline that begins each point.

Service box One of a pair of boxes on either side of the net, between the net and the service lines.

Service line The line on each end of a court that is parallel to the net about halfway between the net and baseline.

Set A group of games won when one player (or team) wins six games by a margin of at least two games. A set can be won with seven games if a tiebreaker is played or if the score is 7–5.

Sideline One of the pair of parallel lines running down both sides of the tennis court. The outer line marks the boundary of the doubles court, and the inner is the boundary of the singles court.

Singles A match in which one player plays against another.

Slice A shot played with a slicing movement under the ball, making it spin backward in the air and bounce low.

Smash *see* **overhead smash**.

Split-step The small jump a player takes as their opponent hits the ball.

Square stance The sideways position for hitting a forehand or backhand stroke. Also called a closed stance.

Take-back The backswing when preparing for a stroke.

Tiebreaker A game played in a match when a set reaches six games all. The first player or team to win seven points (and is at least two points ahead) wins the tiebreaker and the set.

Topspin When a player brings the racket up and over the ball as it is hit, causing it to spin forward in flight and bounce higher than usual.

Volley A shot played before the ball bounces.

Index

Useful information

Tennis organizations

Association of Tennis Professionals (ATP)
201 ATP Boulevard
Ponte Vedra Beach, FL 32082
United States
www.atptennis.com

International Tennis Federation (ITF)
Bank Lane
Roehampton SW15 5XZ
United Kingdom
www.itftennis.com

The Lawn Tennis Association (LTA)
Palliser Road
West Kensington
London W14 9EG
United Kingdom
www.lta.org.uk

Tennis Australia
Private Bag 6060
Richmond South
Victoria 3121
Australia
www. tennisaustralia.com.au

Tennis Canada
3111 Steeles Avenue West
Downsview
ON M3J 3H2
Canada
www.tenniscanada.ca

United States Professional Tennis Association (USPTA)
3535 Briarpark Drive, Suite One
Houston, TX 77042
United States
www.uspta.com

United States Tennis Association (USTA)
70 West Red Oak Lane
White Plains, NY 10604
United States
www.usta.com

Women's Tennis Association (WTA)
One Progress Plaza
Suite 1500
St. Petersburg, FL 33701
United States
www.wtatour.com

World Team Tennis
250 Park Avenue South
9th Floor
New York, NY 10003
United States
www.worldteamtennis.com

Major international tennis tournaments

The Grand Slam
The Grand Slam consists of four annual international open championships:

The Australian Open in January
www.ausopen.org

The French Open in May/June
www.frenchopen.org

The British Open (Wimbledon) in June/July
www.wimbledon.org

The U.S. Open in August/September
www.usopen.org

The Davis Cup
An international team tournament for male professional players. Countries compete against each other in different leagues.
www.daviscup.com

The Fed Cup
An international team tournament for female professional players similar to the Davis Cup.
www.fedcup.com

The **Association of Tennis Professionals (ATP)** runs a series of men's tournaments throughout the year known as the ATP Tour. The **Women's Tennis Association (WTA)** runs the women's tour.

Acknowledgments

Venus and Serena would like to dedicate this book to their parents, Richard Williams and Oracene Price.

Dorling Kindersley would like to thank the following for their help in the preparation and production of this book:

Rene M. Vidal and John Evert from the Evert Tennis Academy, Boca Raton, Florida, for the invaluable technical advice given during the photo shoot; Lisa Queen and Carlos Fleming from IMG for their help and support; all the tennis players who took part in the photo shoot; make-up artist and stylist, Geannin Ramos; Catherine Saunders for her help during the photo shoot; Sharon Weems for her help in organizing the photo shoot; Ransom Everglades School, Florida, for the use of their tennis courts; Mayor Eric Jablin and Kendall Lyon for arranging the use of public courts at Palm Beach Gardens, Florida; and Lisa Lanzarini for directing the Venus and Serena photo shoot.